BATMAN

Exploring the World of Bats

BATMAN

Exploring the World of Bats

LAURENCE PRINGLE

PHOTOGRAPHS BY
MERLIN D. TUTTLE

SCHOLASTIC INC.
New York   Toronto   London   Auckland   Sydney

To Verne and Marion Read,
who helped me to found Bat Conservation International,
with deep appreciation for their many years of
friendship, support, and participation
in my efforts to save the world's bats.

Merlin D. Tuttle

ISBN 0-590-46128-1

Text copyright © 1991 by Laurence Pringle.
Photographs copyright © 1991 by Merlin D. Tuttle.
All rights reserved. Published by Scholastic Inc.,
730 Broadway, New York, NY 10003, by arrangement with
Charles Scribner's Sons Books for Young Readers, Macmillan
Publishing Company.

12 11 10 9 8 7 6 5 4 3 2   3 4 5 6 7 8/9

Printed in the U.S.A.   23

First Scholastic printing, March 1993

The use of *Batman* as the title of this book is by permission of DC Comics Inc. The contents of
this book, however, have no connection with the comic-book character BATMAN.

CONTENTS

ONE

Becoming a Batman

All over the world, people are changing their ideas about bats. Although many bats are still killed out of fear or ignorance, people are learning that bats are harmless, gentle creatures of great value in nature.

More and more, people try to protect bats and even put up special houses to *attract* them. Some kinds of bats are close to extinction, but today there is hope that many of the earth's nearly one thousand species can be saved. This hope, and the change that has begun in public attitudes toward bats, can be credited to one organization, Bat Conservation International, and especially to the scientist who founded it, Merlin Tuttle.

Although Merlin Tuttle's strong interest in bats began almost by accident, he was fascinated by nature at an early age. He was born in Hawaii in 1941. His father was a biology teacher who kept reptiles and amphibians as pets. Both of his parents nurtured his curiosity about nature and that of his younger brother and sister, Arden and Myrna.

One of Merlin's earliest memories is of catching a toad when he was about two years old. His parents let him bring it home and release it near their house. That toad was the first of many animals

A mother Gambian epauleted bat with her pup.

and natural objects that Merlin took home. He collected seashells, butterflies, and all sorts of animals.

When the family moved to northern California, Merlin began to explore wild places and find animals that were new to him. He reared Monarch butterflies and captured shrews and pocket gophers to study. For several summers his father taught a nature education program at Yosemite National Park. Merlin helped catch and raise the young owls, hawks, vultures, magpies, badgers, and other animals that were used in this program.

One school day, a biologist named Ernest Booth spoke to Merlin's class about studying small mammals. He responded to letters from Merlin, who was pleased to learn that a person could actually make a career of studying mammals. Then Merlin's parents gave him a copy of *The Mammals of California,* which in-

Merlin Tuttle, at the age of five, with his parents and brother.

cluded a section on how to do field work. His parents also arranged for him to meet museum scientists, who gave him advice.

At the age of nine, Merlin began to keep a notebook of his wildlife observations. He became increasingly interested in mammals and decided that he would become a mammalogist when he grew up.

In the fifth grade, Merlin demonstrated a characteristic that is still his as an adult. He committed himself to do one thing extremely well. With a passion, Merlin learned as much as he could about the mammals of California. He even memorized their scientific names. Unfortunately, he also failed fifth grade. However, his teachers knew that he could handle the work and let him go on to sixth grade.

In his early teens, Merlin became interested in falconry. With his brother and father, he caught and tamed red-tailed hawks, kestrels, and other hawks. After school he took the birds hunting. One hawk caught rabbits, which Merlin quickly released unharmed. Merlin chuckles as he recalls that the rabbits learned from the experience; after being caught several times, they became too wary to be captured and probably lived longer as a result.

In 1957 the Tuttle family moved to Tennessee, where Merlin attended high school. If they had settled somewhere else—by the ocean, for example—perhaps Merlin's curiosity might have focused on whales or other marine life. But they moved to Knoxville, Tennessee, about two miles from a bat cave.

Merlin noticed that bats visited the cave only in spring and fall. This suggested that the cave was a resting place for migratory bats. However, he had identified the animals as gray bats—a species that all mammal books said was nonmigratory. He continued to observe the gray bats and became more convinced that they migrated somewhere each spring and fall.

In 1958, in his senior year of high school, Merlin persuaded his parents to take him to meet bat experts at the Smithsonian Institution in Washington, D.C. "I brought my three years of observations suggesting that gray bats were migratory, and they gave me several thousand bat bands, saying, 'Here's your chance to prove it.'

"My whole family became involved, and my father spent hundreds of hours helping me capture and band bats. Only a few months after we began banding gray bats, we heard from local old-timers about a cave where bats hibernated. Since it was about a hundred miles north of our home, we doubted its importance to us. We assumed our bats would go south for the winter. Even so, curiosity got the best of us, and by an extreme stroke of luck, we found our banded bats in that cave! They had not only migrated, but they also had gone north instead of south."

By the time Merlin graduated from high school, in 1959, he had completed three studies of bats and shrews that were published in scientific journals. That summer, and for several summers later, the Smithsonian Institution funded his field trips to study bats and other small mammals of the Appalachian Mountains. Assisted by his father, Merlin explored the wilds of several southern states and scores of caves where bats lived.

Merlin enrolled as a freshman in the University of Tennessee. He often cut classes, feeling that his studies of mammals and especially of bats were more important. (The words of Mark Twain come to mind: "I have never let schooling interfere with my education.") His goal was to seek a doctoral degree in mammalogy at the University of Kansas, but that was postponed for a few years. After graduating from Michigan's Andrews University in 1964, Merlin led expeditions for the Smithsonian Institution to study the mammals of Venezuela's rain forests. Eventually, with strong rec-

Merlin, aged twenty-five, with a pet ocelot in Venezuela.

ommendations from several leading mammalogists, in 1968 Merlin Tuttle was accepted as a graduate student by the University of Kansas.

Like many people who are curious about nature, Merlin Tuttle's initial interest had been focused on collecting and identifying living organisms. Now he turned from these "what is it?" questions to the more complex and fascinating "how" and "why" questions about nature. His research subject was the behavior and ecology of gray bats. With his usual dogged determination, he learned a great deal about a little-known bat species.

"One year I scheduled no classes at the university so I was free to make over four hundred trips to bat caves in the southeastern United States. Some of these caves could only be reached by lowering yourself by rope off hundred-foot cliffs." Merlin became a sort of legend among cave explorers as he sought gray bats where no human had ventured before.

In 1974 Merlin Tuttle earned his doctoral degree with honors from the University of Kansas. Now "Dr. Tuttle," he became curator of mammals at the Milwaukee Public Museum. It was a near-perfect job for him, with opportunities to travel and study bats not just in North America but around the world.

Merlin continued to publish the results of his studies in journals. His reputation as a scientist grew, and he became known by many as "batman." (A scientist who specializes in one group of animals sometimes becomes known to his or her colleagues and others as, for example, batman, wolfman, bearman, and in the case of Eugenie Clark, shark woman.)

Merlin enjoyed studying the mammals that he has called "gentle friends" of humans. But he was painfully aware that most people felt differently about bats. His travels took him to many caves and other habitats where bats lived, and he saw that colonies were declining rapidly. This became tragically clear in 1976, when he brought his wife and several friends to see gray bats emerge from Hambrick Cave in Alabama.

This colony of 250,000 bats had been an important part of his doctoral research. Merlin felt emotionally attached to them. He wanted to treat his wife and friends to the spectacle of their flight out of the cave for a night of insect catching. "At almost the same

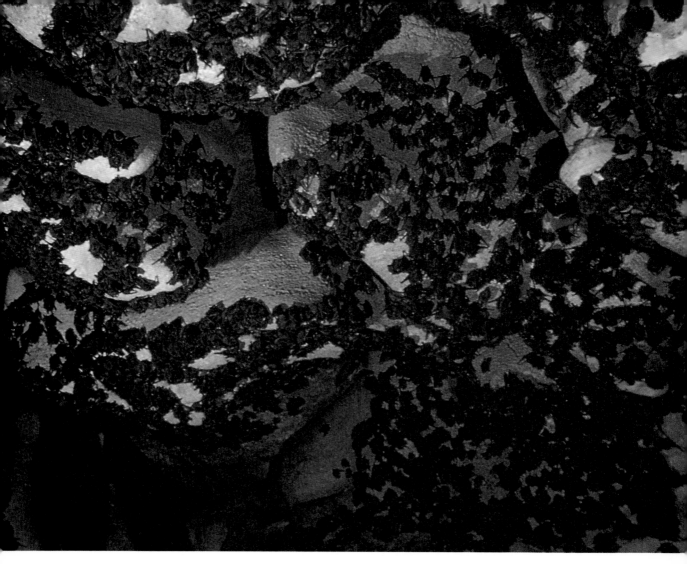

Gray bats roost by the thousands on the ceilings of caves in the south-eastern United States.

time every evening, you could see this big, dark column of bats, 60 feet wide and 30 feet high, going all the way to the horizon. The sound was like a white-water river.

"We were excited," he recalls; "our cameras were ready, but

the bats never came out. Then it dawned on us that the bats were gone. We went into the cave and found sticks, stones, rifle cartridges, and fireworks wrappers beneath what had been a bat roost. There could be no doubt that they had been killed. Many had been banded, and none showed up later in their traditional hibernating caves.

"Hambrick Cave was 5 miles from the nearest human habitation, and you could get there only by boat. It was one of the last places in the world where I expected bats to be destroyed."

Merlin Tuttle felt he had to do something to stop the senseless slaughter of bats. The only hope lay in somehow communicating to the public the truth about bats.

TWO

Getting to Know Real Bats

Bats. To some people, this word means scary, ugly, disease-carrying creatures that are almost blind and sometimes fly into and become entangled in women's hair. These are make-believe bats. Real bats are quite different.

Bats make up nearly a quarter of all mammals on earth and live on all continents except Antarctica. They are the only mammals that fly. "Just as dolphins have mastered the sea," says Merlin Tuttle, "bats have mastered the sky."

There are two main groups of bats. About two hundred species—the megabats—are large, fruit-eating bats called flying foxes. They live in the tropics of Asia and Africa. Some have wingspans of nearly six feet, and others fly about in the daytime, not at night. Flying foxes have big eyes and see very well.

Nearly eight hundred species of small, insect-eating bats make up the second group—the microbats—with forty-two kinds living in Canada and the United States. The smallest mammal on earth is a bat: the bumblebee bat of Thailand. It weighs less than a penny.

Also in this group is a species of bat that catches frogs, one that scoops fish out of the water, others that catch birds and rats, and three species that lap blood from little bites they nip in the

A California leaf-nosed bat swoops down to catch a cricket.

skin of cattle and other warm-blooded prey. These vampire bats live in the warmest regions of South and Central America.

Microbats have small eyes, but they can probably see as well as mice and other small mammals. Their food is mostly flying insects, which they catch in the air at night. To accomplish this a bat flies with its mouth open, emitting high-pitched squeaks that humans cannot hear. Some of the sounds echo off flying insects as well as tree branches and other obstacles that lie ahead. The bat listens to the echoes and gets an instantaneous picture in its brain of the objects in front of it.

With their big eyes, fruit bats are especially appealing. This dwarf epauleted bat from Africa is eating a fig.

From this echolocation, or sonar, as it is called, a bat can tell a great deal about a mosquito or another flying insect. "With extreme precision," Merlin Tuttle says, "bats can perceive motion, distance, speed, trajectory, and shape. They can detect and avoid obstacles no thicker than a human hair, and millions of bats sometimes fly at the same time in a large cave without jamming each other's sonar. Their abilities far surpass our present understanding."

Merlin smiles as he recalls paying a woman twenty dollars to allow him to deliberately put a bat in her hair: "I twisted the hair around and around, and then I let go, and out popped the bat, like a cork from underwater. Bats are far too capable as navigators in the dark to become tangled in anyone's hair."

Some people still shudder at the thought of being face-to-face with a bat. Most of this fear is a result of ignorance about bats and of seeing only images of bats looking their worst, with mouths open and teeth bared. Bats are usually shown this way in advertisement illustrations at Halloween time.

When people are given a chance, they find many bats quite appealing. Flying foxes are named for their resemblance to foxes, which are related to dogs. Almost everyone who gets close to a tame flying fox soon wants to pet and cuddle the bat.

Some microbats do have unusual faces, with large ears and some of the oddest-looking noses in the animal world. This is vital sonar equipment that helps direct and detect the echoes that return to the bats. It enables them to fly deftly, communicate with other bats, and catch food. In short, these features enable the bats to live. They *work* beautifully, and they give bats abilities that we can only admire and hope to understand.

In 1978 Merlin Tuttle began to think about the image that many people have of bats. He was asked to write a chapter about

This gallery of bat faces shows how a straw-colored flying fox (upper left) differs from microbats. It also shows some of the facial features that are a vital part of microbat sonar. The bats are: Chapin's free-tailed bat (upper right), the tent-making bat (lower left), and the spotted bat (lower right).

bats for a book on mammals to be published by the National Geographic Society. Then he saw the photographs that were going to illustrate his words.

Merlin recalls, "I had never considered the impact of the bat pictures that were then typical; most showed bats snarling in self-defense. Because of their shy nature and nocturnal habits, bats are exceptionally difficult to portray photographically as they really are in the wild. When first captured, they either try to fly away, bare their teeth in a threat display, or hunker down, eyes closed, expecting the worst. Impatient photographers typically held a bat by its wings, blew into its face, and snapped a quick picture when the bat tried to defend itself with a snarl."

Photos like these, enlarged and published in books and magazines, reinforced the notion that bats were vicious and fearsome. Merlin wanted his chapter to show bats accurately, and the book editors agreed to try. A *National Geographic* staff photographer, Bates Littlehales, was assigned to take bat photos, under Merlin's direction. After several weeks, however, only a few good photos were taken, despite their best efforts.

Merlin was an amateur photographer when he met Bates Littlehales, who generously shared his knowledge. After Littlehales left to return to *National Geographic,* Merlin began to experiment with the high-speed photography needed to capture bats in flight. When an editor tried to arrange for Littlehales and Tuttle to travel to Mexico to take photos of fishing bats, Littlehales said that Merlin had learned enough about photography to try it alone.

From other mammalogists, Merlin learned where to look in Mexico for fishing bats. After several nights of great effort, he and his assistants caught seven of the bats in nets. The bats became docile after several hours of gentle care but refused to take food.

After much frustration, Merlin was about to give up and re-

When people see only photos of bats baring their teeth in self-defense (left), they may not understand that bats normally look much more appealing (right).

lease the bats, but first he tried tucking bits of cut-up minnow under their lips. Eventually one bat ate a piece of minnow. "Then," Merlin recalls, "to our great elation, he grabbed a whole minnow from my hand, eating it with gusto. The others continued to refuse even small pieces, but we perched them on each side of the feeding bat until, one by one, each succumbed to temptation. An hour later, all seven bats were eagerly eating from our hands and allowing themselves to be photographed with their meals, some in flight.

"When I returned from the trip and had the film developed, I was amazed to see the spectacular photographs that resulted. Even more impressive, when I showed the photographs to others, I soon saw that most people's negative attitudes about bats could be changed in minutes. They simply needed an opportunity to see

Merlin's success at photographing Mexican fishing bats encouraged him to try to film the normal behavior of other species.

bats as they really are. Bats that are not afraid can be just as curious, winsome, and even comical as any household pet."

People who acknowledge that bats are appealing may still fear them because they believe that bats commonly carry the disease rabies. This idea originated in the early 1960s, when research seemed to show that bats were not harmed by rabies, yet passed the deadly disease on to other animals. Further study showed that this was not true, but most people and health officials heard about only the first, erroneous research.

Merlin Tuttle notes that "bats can get rabies, the same as dogs and cats can, but when they do get it they die quickly, just as other animals do. Anyway, less than half of one percent of bats contract rabies, and, unlike most mammals, even when bats are rabid they rarely become aggressive.

"Only about fifteen people in the whole of the United States and Canada are believed to have died of *any* bat-related disease in the past four decades. That's less than the number killed *annually* in the United States alone by dog attacks or from food poisoning contracted at church picnics. When people *are* endangered, it's usually because they've foolishly picked up a sick bat that bites in self-defense."

The greatest threat posed by bats is an indirect one: the actions of unscrupulous or uninformed pest control companies using poisons to kill bats in attics of homes. One widely used poison, chlorophacinone (Rozol), has been clearly shown to pose a serious health threat to people. At least fifteen states still allow its use, and some pest control operators in other states use it illegally.

There are simple, non-chemical ways to keep bats out of houses. Besides, some people are pleased to have a colony of insect-eating bats in or near their homes. "Just leave bats alone," Merlin concludes, "and the odds of being harmed are infinitesimally small."

THREE

Gentle, Intelligent, and Endangered

The positive response to his bat pictures led Merlin Tuttle to devote more time to photography, which complemented his research at the Milwaukee Public Museum. Even today, little is known about most of the world's bats, and the majority have never been photographed alive. In order to take pictures of bats behaving naturally, Merlin first had to learn much about where and how the bats lived.

In 1981 he decided to study frog-eating bats on Panama's Barro Colorado Island. He watched through a special night-vision scope to learn how these bats affect the behavior of courting frogs. His work attracted the curiosity of Michael Ryan, who was studying the courtship behavior of the same frogs that were being caught by bats.

Soon Merlin and Mike joined forces to study how frog calls led bats to their prey. Reporting in the January 1982 issue of *National Geographic,* Merlin wrote, "If the frogs quit calling as soon as a bat comes near, they are safe. Often the hunters pass unwittingly within inches of silent frogs. However, a single faint call, made as a bat approaches, may cost a frog its life."

The scientists played recordings of frog calls and lured frog-

Merlin found that photography complemented his research. In order to take pictures of bats, he had to learn much about their normal behavior.

eating bats into fine-meshed nets, called mist nets, that are used to catch bats in flight. After gently taming the bats, they put them in a large outdoor cage and tested their responses to the recorded calls of different kinds of frogs. Frog-eating bats, they discovered, could distinguish between the calls of edible frogs and poisonous frogs. They avoided the latter. They could also tell the difference between the calls of frogs of edible size and those that were too big to eat.

Tuttle and Ryan were able to verify their findings by playing frog calls at ponds in the wild. However, to take close-up pictures of bats catching frogs, Merlin set up a natural-looking tabletop pond and trained bats to swoop down on their prey at his command.

He was amazed at the bats' intelligence: "Frog-eating bats could be trained in as little as two hours from the time of capture to come to my hand when I called. Perhaps even more remarkable, they also could be trained to respond to simple hand signals alone."

Taking advantage of the bats' quick intelligence, Merlin was able to focus his camera on a specific frog perched by the water, then point to the frog. On cue, a trained bat flew in from a predictable direction and grabbed the frog in its mouth as its photo was taken.

Following this success, Merlin Tuttle has since captured and trained other kinds of bats in order to take pictures of them catching prey, pollinating flowers, or doing other natural activities. His teenage experiences of taming and training hawks for falconry no doubt contributed to his success as a wildlife photographer. A few people were disappointed to learn that some of the bats in his photos have been tamed and trained. But most are even more impressed to find that bats are so intelligent.

Those who think photography of captive bats is easy, Merlin says, "may be interested to learn that even with trained bats on an artificial set, I often take a hundred or more pictures to get just one suitable for publication. Without taming and sometimes training wild bats for photography, their world would forever remain shrouded in mystery and misunderstanding for all but a few privileged scientists.

"The bats are harmlessly netted, gently handled, and released as quickly as possible. Often it's more difficult to say 'good-bye' than to get acquainted. I'd like to think that many of my favorite

A frog-eating bat in Panama pinpoints its prey by listening to a frog's calls.

bat friends are still alive and happy out there in some deep dark jungle night."

On a photographic expedition, Merlin carries about three hundred and fifty pounds of equipment, including several cameras and tripods, many lenses, and up to fifteen flash units and their stands. He has taken pictures of over three hundred species of bats worldwide. Vehicles and photographic equipment have been damaged, but Merlin has so far avoided serious injury while venturing into caves, abandoned mines, hollow trees, and other places where bat colonies live. He has taken some risks, staying out alone to catch bats in an area of Thailand where tigers sometimes kill people, and crawling into caves where he found the cast-off skins of large cobras.

Nearly everywhere Merlin has traveled he has found bats in trouble. Cave explorers often told him, "No bats live in here."

As night falls in Utah, Merlin sets up a fine-meshed mist net that catches flying bats without harm.

Thousands of Mexican free-tailed bats emerge from their cave and begin a nightly hunt for flying insects.

They were right, but Merlin would dig into the cave floors and find old bones and deposits of guano (bat body wastes). Bats *had* lived there; now they were gone.

Chemical pesticides and deliberate killing have reduced many bat populations. In Asia and the Pacific islands, hunting and netting of flying foxes for food have already caused the extinction of several species. In the New World, the biggest colony ever known, at Eagle Creek Cave in Arizona, numbered thirty million Mexican free-tailed bats in 1963. People fired shotguns into roosting clusters of these harmless, insect-eating bats. Now there are fewer than thirty thousand.

"Bats," Merlin explained, "are uniquely easy to kill. They group in large, vulnerable formations and are the slowest-reproducing mammals for their size on earth. Although some bats may live more than thirty years, a mother bat usually rears just one pup a year. A colony or species that is much reduced in number is at great risk. The survival of each pup is critical, and a long period of protection is needed for the bats to recover."

Amateur cave explorers are a major cause of declining bat populations. In the summer, baby bats cluster in special places in caves where the climate is just right for their comfort. Scared by people, their mothers may move them to a place in the cave that is more sheltered but too cold for survival. Merlin Tuttle has seen caves where a single disturbance by people caused 60 percent or more of the pups to die.

Hibernating bats are also vulnerable. In the United States and other areas with cold winters, bats must survive for several months without feeding. Their body temperatures drop low, and they scarcely breathe. They rely on stored fat to survive the winter. Disturbed by cave visitors, bats begin to raise their body temperature in preparation for escape. This costs the bats between ten and thirty days of their stored fat reserve. If people repeatedly enter bat caves in winter, entire populations of hibernating bats can exhaust their fat reserves and die.

When Merlin Tuttle began bat research in earnest, as a teenager in the 1950s, professional mammalogists unwittingly harmed bat colonies by entering caves in winter to band the bats. Now the danger of disturbing bats both in winter and in the pup-rearing season has been recognized. Many experienced cave explorers (who usually are members of the National Speleological Society)

If mother bats are disturbed, they often move their pups to less desirable locations where they may not survive.

know which caves can be explored without harm to bats. Unfortunately, many amateur cave explorers still have no idea of their devastating impact on the fragile life cycles of bats.

In the late 1970s, the gray bat and several other bats were listed as endangered species in the United States—thanks to the efforts of Merlin Tuttle and a few other concerned ecologists. Tuttle approached several environmental organizations and urged them to take up the cause of bats. He was told that the cause was hopeless: bats were too unpopular.

Then and now, conservation groups have found it is much easier to raise money to help save wild animals that most people find appealing. (For the same reason, most animal welfare groups pay more attention to dogs and chimpanzees than to rats and chickens.) Merlin Tuttle knew that bats were not "glamour" animals, that most people would rather send money to help pandas than bats. But he also believed that "cute and cuddly has nothing to do with intrinsic value."

In 1979 Merlin Tuttle attended a meeting of bat experts in England. Afterward he toured the study sites of his friend Robert Stebbings, a British "batman." They discussed the worldwide decline in bat populations and the difficulty of getting people interested.

The only hope, it seemed, was to create a new organization. Bat Conservation International was formed in 1982.

FOUR

Meeting the Challenge of Bat Conservation

"**I**magine what it's like," says Merlin Tuttle, "to start an organization whose sole purpose is conservation of one of the least popular groups of animals on earth."

Bat Conservation International began as a part-time effort, added to Merlin's work as curator of mammals at the Milwaukee Public Museum. A brochure called "Why Save Bats?" was printed and used to raise funds and attract members. Another, "Bats and Public Health," helped answer the questions of numerous people who were misinformed about this matter.

After four years, in 1986, membership was about a thousand people in twenty-two countries. But the organization was growing rapidly both in members and influence. The news media, tired of the same old "scary bat" stories, were intrigued by a respected scientist who said that bats were nothing to be afraid of—and something to appreciate.

Merlin Tuttle's credibility as a batman and his photos encouraged increasing numbers of people to reconsider their ideas about bats. In more than one instance he played a key role in gaining protection for large bat colonies.

In 1982 Merlin checked on the status of a cave in Florida that was a nursery for many thousands of gray bats and other species. He was alarmed to learn that the forested land around the cave had been sold and that the owner planned a housing development for the site.

Merlin called the developer and told him he owned one of the most important bat caves in eastern North America. Now it was the owner's turn to be upset. He wanted to get rid of the bats as quickly as possible.

Merlin knew that just ten minutes' work with a bulldozer would cover the cave entrance and wipe out the bats. He recalls, "The owner seemed to feel that he was talking to a kook, and I tried to think of some way to change his ideas about bats. I asked him if he subscribed to *National Geographic.* He did. Then I asked if he had ordered the National Geographic Society's book *Wild Animals of North America.* Luckily, he had, and he agreed to read my chapter on bats before taking any action on the bat cave."

When Merlin called the next day, the developer was impressed but still was concerned about the possibility of bats spreading rabies. Merlin flew to Florida, bringing a copy of "Bats and Public Health" to dispel needless fears.

"I showed the developer the cave and caught a couple of gray bats. We took them back to his house, and soon his children were petting them. We went back to the cave in the evening and watched the huge colony stream out, up through the forest, and into the sky. The family was enthralled."

Taking a financial loss, the developer sold the cave area and a buffer zone of land around it to the Nature Conservancy. The nursery cave is now protected by the state of Florida, and bats still nurse their young there and consume tons of mosquitoes and other insects.

Bat Conservation International now has helped gain protec-

The Florida cave that was threatened by a housing development is home to thousands of insect-eating gray bats.

tion for many important bat colonies in the United States and abroad. The value of bats as insect eaters certainly contributed to these successes. They are the only major predators of nocturnal flying insects, including many pests of crops, gardens, and yards. Merlin Tuttle has calculated that the twenty million free-tailed bats of Bracken Cave in Texas can eat nearly a half million pounds of insects in a single night.

Although many kinds of bats will feast on mosquitoes if they

are especially abundant, different species usually seek favorite foods. Some feed mostly on beetles, others on moths. Pallid bats snatch grasshoppers, katydids, and even scorpions from vegetation or the ground.

When little brown bats were released in a room full of mosquitoes, they each caught up to six hundred in an hour. Little brown bats are one species of a group, called mouse-eared bats, that is widespread in North America. They are common in Chautauqua, a summer cultural resort in western New York where bats have been respected and protected for decades.

Merlin visited Chautauqua one summer. "My hosts credited bats for the town's scarcity of mosquitoes, and I was, of course, curious to see for myself. For three summer evenings I walked Chautauqua's streets and enjoyed its outdoor amphitheater; sure enough, I wasn't bitten a single time. At dusk thousands of bats could be seen hunting, more than I have seen in any other town in eastern North America. The only insect I noticed was caught by a bat within seconds."

At Chautauqua and all across North America, people are putting up specially designed wooden houses for bats. The houses are open at the bottom. This makes them useless for birds or squirrels, but fine for bats, which cling to inside surfaces. Bat Conservation International sells bat houses and also provides plans for people who want to build their own.

When bat populations are wiped out, insect pests multiply. This occurred in Israel, where the government poisoned caves to kill fruit bats and killed most of the nation's insect-eating bats. Moth populations exploded, and moth caterpillars became major agricultural pests. Now growers use expensive chemical pesticides

Pallid bats of the western United States and Mexico fly close to the ground, catching scorpions and large insects.

to accomplish pest control that bats once provided for free.

In Israel and in many other nations, fruit bats are killed because growers believe that they seriously damage their crops. However, research shows this is rarely true. Flying foxes seldom eat fruit that is not completely ripe, and commercial growers pick fruit before it is ripe. This is the case in Kenya, Africa, where mangoes are picked for shipment to markets several days prior to ripening. Nevertheless, many growers believe that fruit bats are pests on their plantations. People in Kenya have sealed the openings of caves and destroyed many bat populations.

Merlin Tuttle went to Kenya in 1985 to investigate the matter. He visited fifteen mango farms over a wide area. "I learned to identify the tooth marks of a variety of animals and examined nearly 7,500 mangoes for damage. When harvestable mangoes were harmed, the culprits were nearly always monkeys, not bats."

Merlin also offered unripe mangoes, bananas, papayas, and other fruits to six species of flying foxes he captured. The bats were kept in a net enclosure for eighteen hours. They were hungry but refused to eat the unripe fruits. When finally offered ripe fruits they gobbled them down. Merlin concluded "bats apparently do not like unripe fruit any more than people do."

Flying foxes may actually perform a service for growers by eating ripe fruits left after harvest. By doing so they also deprive of food the larvae of harmful fruit flies and reduce the numbers of these pests.

Bat researchers have discovered that fruit-eating bats play a vital role in spreading tree seeds in rain forests. The seeds pass through their digestive tracts, are expelled in flight, and help regenerate forests that have been cut. Flying foxes seem to be the only seed dispersers of one important timber tree, the iroko of

The hammerheaded bat of Africa carries countless thousands of seeds that are essential to rain forest regrowth.

West Africa. According to Merlin, "Seeds dropped by bats can account for up to 95 percent of forest regrowth on cleared land."

Many tropical trees and shrubs are pollinated by nectar-feeding bats that visit the flowers at night. Plants often have a "lock-and-key" relationship with animals, with specially adapted flower colors, odors, and shapes that attract them and enable them to spread pollen from one plant to another.

In his book *America's Neighborhood Bats,* Merlin Tuttle wrote, "We already know that more than three hundred plant species in the Old World tropics alone rely on the pollinating and seed dispersal services of bats, and additional bat-plant relationships are constantly being discovered. These plants provide more than four hundred and fifty economically important products, valued in the hundreds of millions of dollars. Just one, the durian fruit of Southeast Asia, sells for $120 million each year and relies almost exclusively on flying foxes for pollination."

In the southwestern United States and Mexico, long-nosed bats are the main pollinators of several important plants, including large organ-pipe and saguaro cacti. The bats' especially long noses and tongues enable them to get nectar from these plants.

Long-nosed bats were recently listed as endangered species. If they were to die out, much more than a species of bat might disappear. The bats are sometimes referred to as a "keystone" species by ecologists. The giant cacti they pollinate provide food and shelter for countless other animals. Without the bats, Merlin Tuttle said, "These majestic plants and the wildlife that rely on them could be seriously threatened."

Other kinds of bats are keystone species in South America, Asia, and Africa. In 1989, Merlin wrote, "On the savannas of East Africa, the giant baobab is known as the "Tree of Life" because so many other plants and animals depend on it for survival. But the tree itself depends on bats. Its showy white flowers open only at night and are specially adapted to be pollinated by bats. Without bats, the baobab could die out, triggering a chain of linked extinctions and threatening plant and animal life throughout the region.''

The vital role of bats in nature is not well known, and a tragic

The lesser long-nosed bat is a primary pollinator of the giant saguaro cactus. Such plants must have animal pollinators in order to produce seeds.

slaughter of many species continues. In Australia, flying foxes are pollinators of many economically important plants, but "bat shoots" have wiped them out over large areas. In parts of Asia these large bats are highly prized as food. The island of Guam once had two species of flying foxes. Now one is extinct and the other is nearly gone, a result of being hunted too much for food.

A member of Bat Conservation International, botanist Paul Cox, learned that flying foxes were being wiped out by hunters on American Samoa, a United States territory located about twenty-three hundred miles southwest of Hawaii. On its five islands Samoa is home to two species of flying foxes.

In 1985 Paul Cox requested help from Bat Conservation International and was soon joined in Samoa by Merlin Tuttle and fellow bat conservationists Verne and Marion Read. They studied the situation and met with government leaders.

As a result of their visit, Samoa's government has since outlawed commercial hunting of bats. In 1989 Samoan flying foxes were given further protection when nearly eighty-five hundred acres were set aside to become a national park. This will be the first tropical rain forest protected by the U.S. National Park Service. Although Samoan leaders were strongly in favor of having the park, Bat Conservation International played a major role in its creation. For more than two years, its staff and many members wrote letters, made telephone calls, and testified at hearings in order to gain needed support in the U.S. Congress for the park.

In 1990 Bat Conservation International had a staff of fifteen at its headquarters in Austin, Texas. Merlin had decided to move to Texas in 1986, when the staff was just himself and a secretary. "It was scary," he recalls, "to leave a secure museum job to run a conservation organization. My income was cut nearly in half, and we had no office equipment but were given office space at the

University of Texas. Within a year, however, our membership and financial support had grown so that we were able to find larger quarters, which we needed for a growing staff."

Although Merlin had regrets about leaving his research position at the Milwaukee Public Museum, as a batman he was pleased to move from a state with eight species of bats to one with thirty-two. Texas is home to more kinds of bats than any other state. Bracken Cave, site of the world's biggest bat colony, is a short drive from Austin.

Austin also attracted Merlin because it represented a challenge. He had noticed a stream of antibat news stories from there, and, when he arrived, learned that people wanted to poison the large colony of bats that had become established in downtown Austin. The Congress Avenue Bridge had been remodeled, and the structural changes provided ideal roosting places for nearly a million free-tailed bats. Austin had inadvertently become the summer home of the world's largest urban bat population.

Bat Conservation International soon dispelled the notion that the bats were a health threat, and Austin citizens learned that their bats could eat from fifteen thousand to thirty thousand pounds of insects on a single night. Before long the bats were seen as a community asset. Now hundreds of people gather to watch the bats emerge at twilight. Travel agents report that the bats have become a tourist attraction. And the city government has built an educational exhibit about bats near the bridge. Austin now celebrates the return of its bats each summer.

In Bat Conservation International's booklet *Bats: Gentle Friends, Essential Allies,* a map shows places all over the world where the organization has helped change ideas about bats and helped bat populations. In Thailand, Merlin Tuttle advised a community on how to protect bats from poachers. A monastery, a

Residents and tourists gather to watch the spectacle of free-tailed bats emerging from their summer home under Austin's Congress Avenue Bridge.

school with about four hundred and fifty pupils, and many townspeople depended on the bats in Khao Chong Pran Cave for survival. People collect bat guano, a valuable fertilizer, and sell it for vital income. The guano harvest had dropped, however, as hunters killed more and more bats to sell as food. Following Merlin's advice, the community hired a guard for the cave. The bat population is recovering, and income from guano is greater than ever before.

One bat conservation story that gives Merlin special pleasure is that of Hambrick Cave in Alabama. He still remembers the shock of discovering, in 1976, that its quarter million bats were dead. After taking action to have the gray bat protected as an

38

endangered species, Merlin persuaded the Tennessee Valley Authority (TVA), which owned the cave site, to protect any bats that settled there.

The cave entrance is in a cliff face by the shore of a TVA lake. The TVA drove pilings into thirty feet of water as part of a fence that keeps people, but not bats, out. And gray bats have reestablished a thriving colony in Hambrick Cave.

By 1990 Bat Conservation International's membership had grown to more than ten thousand in fifty-five countries and was increasing rapidly. It had accomplished a lot in a few years. But

In Thailand, reducing the capture of too many bats for food allowed the colony to grow and increased the harvest of guano for fertilizer.

the plight of bats around the world keeps Merlin Tuttle on a hectic schedule of studying bats, taking photographs, and trying to educate fruit growers, government officials, and others on the value of bats. The years 1989 and 1990 were especially busy as he traveled all over the world, guiding the filming of a television documentary about bats. He spoke excitedly about the film, about slow-motion close-ups of bats catching mosquitoes, pollinating flowers, and much more. This extraordinary film will be shown in more than a hundred nations, and many millions of people for the first time will see what real bats are like.

Merlin Tuttle is modest about his accomplishments in bat conservation. "It is almost addicting," he says, "to see what one person can do. But I've succeeded because I was able to marshal tremendous support for Bat Conservation International. There are growing numbers of people who realize that even unappealing animals can be invaluable in nature. They recognize that we need bats, whether we like them or not, and many now like them, as well."

People tend to fear animals they haven't met and don't understand. Thanks to Merlin Tuttle's photographs, his research, and his conservation efforts, many people are meeting bats and learning about them. At last, they are beginning to appreciate and even like our planet's gentle, beneficial bats.

FURTHER READING

Ackerman, Diane. "Bats." *The New Yorker,* February 29, 1988, pp. 37–62.

Bat Conservation International (BCI). *Bats: Gentle Friends, Essential Allies.* Austin, Texas: Bat Conservation International, 1988. (A 16-page, color-illustrated, 8½- by 11-inch booklet available from BCI, P.O. Box 162603, Austin, Texas 78716.)

Cooper, Gale. "Bat Conservation International." In *Animal People.* Boston: Houghton Mifflin, 1983 (pps. 127–134).

McCracken, Gary, and Mary Gustin. "Batmom's Daily Nightmare." *Natural History,* October 1987, pp. 66–72.

Novacek, Michael. "Navigators of the Night." *Natural History,* October 1988, pp. 66–71.

Pringle, Laurence. *Vampire Bats.* Hillside, N.J.: Enslow Publishers, 1982.

Tuttle, Merlin. "The Amazing Frog-Eating Bat." *National Geographic,* January 1982, pp. 78–91.

———. *America's Neighborhood Bats: Understanding and Learning to Live in Harmony with Them.* Austin: University of Texas Press, 1988.

———. "Gentle Fliers of the African Night." *National Geographic,* April 1986, pp. 540–556.

———. "Harmless, Highly Beneficial, Bats Still Get a Bum Rap." *Smithsonian,* January 1984, pp. 74–81.

———. "Photographing the World's Bats: Adventure, Tribulation, and Rewards." *Bats,* Winter 1988, pp. 4–9.

———. "Texas Bats: A Resource in Peril." *Texas Parks and Wildlife,* April 1989, pp. 2–7.

INDEX